Connecting Entrepreneurs, Philanthropists and Influencers.

BUSINESS

BOOSTER TODAY MAGAZINE

THE #1 GERMANY BASED MAGAZINE FOR THE GLOBAL ENTREPRENEUR

DEAN GRAHAM
SALES, BRANDING & POSITIONING AUTHORITY

THE SUCCESS CREATORS
GLOBAL TOUR

CHRISTIAN BARTSCH
TOP 100 CEO BUSINESS COACH

VOL. 2 | NO. 6 |
JULY 2019

CONTENT

SECTIONS

CONNECT WITH US

Read more Business Booster Today Magazine content at BusinessBoosterToday.com

Download the **Business Booster Today App** for iPhone or Android.

Like the **Business Booster Today Magazine on Facebook** for the latest news, photos, videos and exclusive online content.

Follow **@mybbtmagazine** on Twitter and keep informed on breaking news and business trends.

View stories and photos on Instagram and get a backstage insight. Follow us at **businessboostertoday**

Make connections with fellow entrepreneurs and business people in our community at businessboostertoday.com

FOUNDERS CORNER

By Sue Baumgärtner-Bartsch

One year ago, we started this magazine with the vision to empower 20 million people to grow and explode their business and boost their life, business and profit to greater heights and space.

What started out as an online Magazine first, turned into a printed magazine and now into a digitalized airline magazine that is flying around the world, reaching 160mio passengers and +300k luxury hotels.

Business Booster Today magazine has been named the #1 German Magazine for the Global Entrepreneur. Boom!!! Although we are based in Munich Germany, the world has truly become our home.

We are excited and humble by all the amazing people we meet, entrepreneurs we are inspiring and the movers and shakers of the business world who are making an impact. Connecting people, places, and even continents is what we are doing with this magazine, with the passion to changing lives and businesses, and with the perseverance to think big and make the impossible possible.

We work with and support key note speakers, coaches, entrepreneurs and those who align with our vision of entrepreneurship, freedom of life and business. What makes our magazine unique is that we have a magazine from entrepreneurs for entrepreneurs.

In order to increase your business, leads and impact, it is critical to be branded. Branding does not cost you any money, branding makes you money.

Become branded by being in magazines and getting your story and mission into the press. Nothing comes for free in this world. It is the people you surround yourself with that makes a huge impact on your well-being. Let's focus on wisdom, integrity, collaboration and freedom as entrepreneurs to make an even bigger impact together. Together we succeed, and together we can make an even greater impact!

IMPRESS

ISSN (Print Edition)

2627-9223

ISSN (Online Edition)

2627-9231

PUBLICATION DATE

01.07.2019

PUBLICATION SERIES INFO

July 2019 No. 6

PUBLICATION REVISION ID

2019-06-26--1

PUBLISHER & EDITOR IN CHIEF

Christian Bartsch

LEAD EDITOR & VP

Sue Baumgaertner-Bartsch

CONTRIBUTING EDITORS

Udo Bartsch, Douglas Vermeeren, Melody Garcia, Jan Erik Horgen, Michael Knulst, Louis Kotze, Marina Kotze, Sylvija Popovic, John Stokoe, Eren Ünlü, Greg JC Granier

CONTRIBUTING WRITERS

Michelle Davis, Robb Evans, Billy Gajic, Raluca Gomeaja, Sam Komeha, Katrin Israel, Jaine Lopez, Vikas Malkani, Robert Martin, Danijela Nakovski, Milos Nakovski, Christine Nielsen, Jim Paar, Nina Peutherer, Richard Peutherer, Gavin Sim, Nina Schmid, Kirstie Shapiro, Stefanos Sifandos, Tomer Sapir Spitkowski, Cristina Stavinski, Mona Tenjo, Janine Van Throo, Yasemin Yazan, Brett Yeager, Erwin Wils , Sabine Zettl

PHOTOGRAPHY

Dalibor Kojic & Editors & Advertisers

VIP STYLING & MAKEUP

Aldrin-David Verburgt

PUBLISHED BY

ACATO GmbH, 1st. Floor, Theresienhoehe 28, 80339 Munich, Germany

ADVERTISING & SALES

sales@businessboostertoday.com

Phone +49 89 54041070

www.businessboostertoday.com

SUBSCRIPTIONS

Booster club members: annual membership dues include €197 for a regular one-year subscription and €47 for an electronic member subscription. Non-members subscription rate are €97 for an electronic subscription. Change of address notices and subscriptions should be directed to BBT magazine.

EDITORIAL TEAM

THE MOVERS AND SHAKERS
THE DREAM TEAM

Christian Bartsch

Publisher &

Editor in Chief

Sue Baumgärtner-Bartsch

VP & Interview Editor

Melody Garcia

Philanthropy Editor

John Stokoe

Property Editor

Douglas Vermeeren

Leadership Editor

Eren Ünlü

Technology Editor

Orsi Beata Nagy

Business Processes
Editor

Silvija Popovic

Mindset Editor

Michael Knulst

Business Editor

Udo Bartsch

Business Editor

Jan Erik Horgen

Investment Editor

Louis Kotze

Language Editor

Melody Garcia

Philanthropy Editor

Greg JC Granier

Entertainment Industry
Editor

Marina Kotze

Health Editor

Dalibor Kojic

Photographer

Aldrin-David Verburgt

VIP Stylist

Gábor Dobos

VIP & Stage
Photographer

INTERVIEW WITH THE FOUNDERS OF "THE SUCCESS CREATORS": CHRISTIAN BARTSCH & DEAN GRAHAM

By Sue Baumgaertner-Bartsch (Germany)

The Success Creators Dean Graham from South Africa and Christian Bartsch from Germany share their insights when it comes to making a global impact as entrepreneurs.

Sue BB: Dean, you are a global personal branding and positioning expert, international speaker and venture entrepreneur. Can you share with us your definition on personal branding and why it matters?

Dean G: For years, I have looked at the markets and brands that grow and continually grow, and it's always the brands with people behind them that have the best and fastest growth. People like to see a face behind a product or service.

When someone is personally branded, they provide credibility to their product. Your brand needs to be congruent but how you position your brand is key. A lot of branding companies focus too much on the content and too little on the positioning and timing.

Sue BB: People have seen you doing business and speaking in many different parts of the world. What made you seek entrepreneurial journey rather than stay in the corporate world?

Dean G: I got sick of making other people rich, making their dreams happen with my blood sweat and tears. The day I realized I can sell sand in a dessert; it was an easy decision. Why take 25% of profits when you can make the entire amount yourself and expand.

Sue BB: Christian, you have a strong business and IT background and people call you "The Top 100 Business CEO Coach". Please share with us a bit about your background, and why that is.

Chris B: As an experienced IT Entrepreneur & International

Marketing Expert I have experience from multiple industries (BMW, KPMG, Siemens) and countries (DE, CA, UK).

My background is with BMW HQ (Germany) on Automotive Business Management and on Dealership Management in Sydney (Australia). I then studied IT at the Munich University of Applied Science (Germany) and then Management at the Monash University (Australia).

I have years of experience of setting up companies in different countries, launching businesses in areas that are dominated by larger entities and finding the niche where these businesses can focus on growing a stable client base. I had to deal with all the great and not so great sides of being in businesses.

As a business coach and consultant, I work with different businesses and leaders in an international environment, and I help them find the right solutions, so their business

about, and it started early on. As a child, we were living in many different parts of the world, so I had to adapt quickly to new people, cultures and later on in business. Being passionate and doing something with joy will help you to excel in whatever you do.

For me flying is like broadening your horizon and widening your perspective. You need to have this power skill of 1) seeing through things and 2) looking far into the future as well. These are what I call my super powers. You have to develop them and grow them to succeed in life and in business.

The key to success is to never give up by being determined against all odds.

Sue BB: Dean, what is your set of core values and business skills that have helped you in your career and why?

Dean G: Honesty and loyalty. Always be honest with your clients. They will understand and they in turn will provide you with loyalty. Always under promise and over deliver, most companies promise the world and provide an average service.

Sue BB: You both are global entrepreneurs, and you have been dealing with different people, behaviors, cultures and socio-economic backgrounds. Forming partnerships and collaborations is one aspect that helps people step up from being a solopreneur to doing business on a global scale. Why do some business partnerships work better than others in your opinion?

Dean G: Forming a partnership can definitely help you grow faster when the partnership lines up with your business and similar target market.

Entrepreneurs are always under the impression that when they form a partnership its easy business, but if you and the partner are not aligned this will only waste valuable time. And a lot of times this will affect

can grow from unstock to speed mode. I am used to solving problems and finding creative solutions since I was a child.

Sue BB: Christian, what does it take to succeed in business? Is it the people we meet, celebrities, Is it passion- what is it?

Chris B: This reminds me actually of a funny story. I was 2 years old and at the airport with my parents and James Last was there with a drink on his table. I must have thought it was water, went to him and drank it all down. I slept like a baby but yes, that was my first encounter with a celebrity. Travelling and flying is what I am absolutely passionate

CHRISTIAN BARTSCH
IT-Spezialist

n·tv

The purpose of this book is empower kasi entrepreneurs to manage and profit from their busi-

Success is a poor teacher!
Graham visits Mzansi to motivate youth to fail and learn!

South Africans were privileged to host Dean Graham, a world well known successful entrepreneur and speaker in renowned business events around the World.

Graham is not just an entrepreneur but an advocate for the youth in becoming entrepreneurs, as opposed merely seeking employment. *Mapepeza* correspondent, Lerato Phosisi interviewed Dean during his short stay in Mzansi recently.

Dean uses his own experience of failures, trials and hardships as the backbone of his teachings. He shows young people exactly the errors they need to be aware of and to avoid in particular when it comes to entrepreneurship.

He firmly believes that success is a poor teacher when it comes to business and careers.

"We give basics sales skills, using real scenarios and teaching them that failure is an option they can use to bounce back and become a success.

"I tried to work but realised at some stage that I have the ability to sell.

Then I got into direct selling (for commission). Later, I got sick from taking 20% and making the other person rich. Then my journey of entrepreneurship started and ever since it has never stopped," said Graham.

"I always like to advise kids to start at an early age, from either 10 or 13 years old, in working on whatever they want to be in life.

They shouldn't wait to be 40 years in order to decide on the career of their choice and start the journey. If you're going to fail, fail a lot and do it while young because failure is a learning curve," he said.

Dean Graham said he attributes his business success to learning from his shortcomings. He currently runs five firms. "Failing is fantastic. I have failed many times to be were I am today. Most people think having money is the reward to success in businesss. But failure is the part of life that enables one in becoming the best.

If you do not fail, you will forever be average and you can only follow everyone else," he said.

deliverables in the end costing you credibility and money.

So, in a nutshell you need to find a mutually beneficial partnership that both sides can go to market with and add value to each other's services/products without detracting from their core business activities.

Chris B: No one has created an empire by themselves. It is through collaborations and partnerships that we grow and create a bigger impact in this world. Innovative ideas are great when you have them, but then you need people to implement them. Teamwork is key, and finding the right people to team up with.

It all comes down to integrity, honesty and creating synergies. That means find those people and work with those who complement your skill set.

When you do business, you fail but I do not call it failure, I call it learning. So, I have learnt a great deal about people, behaviors of people and those who talk bullshit and want to take your money.

My advice is to always team up with somebody you can trust and shares your set of core values, and do not go into a deal because of the money only. I do not work with someone who is ego-driven, but I partner with people who show commitment, care and who truly want to create, innovate or change something for the better.

I believe that TOGETHER we can boost lives and businesses to greater heights, profits and space. ✒

HOW TO FIGHT LONELINESS AS AN ENTREPRENEUR

By Raluca Gomeja (France)

Studies show a high psychological impact on personal life of entrepreneurs which was linked with their business success.

And it makes sense as it is more likely to be affected higher by our work when this is our own business than when we work for an organization/someone else. Adding the fact that entrepreneurship comes along in numerous situations with either working alone, or **feeling very lonely** while **fulfilling the role of business owner**, even when having some small teams. It is therefore absolutely normal for most of entrepreneurs to identify themselves with their businesses.

Saying that, and providing you reading this as an entrepreneur or one to become, here are a few reminders on **how to keep the distance** between what happens in your business and *what impact that has on your life.*

1. Your business is not your life. For some it may be your purpose, yet it is not your life

2. When your business fails, it is not your personal failure. You did create a business and you can create a second one.

3. Fixing business goals is good as long as you don't measure yourself as a person based on achieving those. Detach from the outcome.

4. Your happiness and fulfilment depend on many factors, not only your business success. Meaning that the old work-life balance topic is even more of a topic when you run your own business

5. In our minds we are always right. Meaning we will find the right reason or logic for us to do what we do, including for the "sacrifices" we need to do.

So yes, this may or will happen to most entrepreneurs. We can see problems as blockers, or we can see problems as sources for solutions. What solutions do we have?

1. Speak out. Showing vulnerability is not a weakness. You can choose to fake it till you make it, yet, any business person is first a person, not a machine or a robot. That comes

with feelings as well. It is absolutely normal for a business owner to **feel down when something bad happens** in his/her business. Keeping it inside, or even pretend that we are not affected is not working. At the end of the day those feelings will reach out in much more brutal ways like depression, serious illnesses, and nervous breakdown or burnout.

2. Be part of a like-minded community of entrepreneurs. They have been there already, some solutions are obvious yet not visible when we run the business. We can't see the picture from the frame. Why not get some of these solutions out from some other business people experience for example. Don't only focus on what network events do I attend to increase my business figures, focus also on what network events do I need to create a support system for myself and others.

3. Create your own administration board, so you can benefit from an objective view of what is happening in your business.

4. Make sure you add something else into your life than just one business, meaning do not build a business which takes away your life, build a business who adds to your life. Easier said than done, yet this is when coaches, consultants and mentors are really great to work with. Working with the right coach will not be a cost but a real save of

time, energy and money.

5. Know what motivates you. I will not lie to you: the first years of the business, the business will take over, it is hard work so very little time remains for something else. Yet here we don't talk about time, we talk about energy. We can tell when someone's work energizes them. So choose something that is bringing value to people and markets (that is a must in any business models), and also that brings energy to you as a person. Before launching any business step back and ask yourself why. Because if we link expectations of fulfillment, joy, happiness and freedom to a business we may as well be disappointed and frustrated. A business can and will bring those moments, yet they may not be the right reasons to start a business.

The **entrepreneurial journey** is <u>not a walk in a park on a sunny day</u>, yet it is not a permanent nightmare either. The key like everything in life is to know your why and improve yourself every day. There will be bad times, a lot, and good times, a few. Yet those good times are worth it. And you can do this.

"Alone we walk fast, together we walk far"- African proverb.

SPEAKER PACKAGE FOR ONLY €9900

Includes the following benefits

- Full Media biography design

- Become an International Speaker

- Gain media exposure & mass visibility on Multiple TV. Radio, Magazine interviews (valued at €40 000.00)

- The Award winners will get further TV and radio Exposure. as well as a cover story with 4 page article in a renown magazine

- First option to attend other international Legacy events

- Includes 7 night's accommodation and a private chauffeur to and from Venue

- There will be an awards dinner on the last day, Awards will be after the event at a gala dinner.

We can help with flights and accommodation as well as transport to and .from the event. Speakers will get ultimate credibility to build their brand and speaking engagements. The coach will also get the number 1 speaker coach if their client wins.

For more details visit:
www.legacyentrepreneurssummit.com

THE 'HUMANIZATION' OF BUSINESS

By Stefanos Sifandos (USA & Europe)

Times are evolving and changing. The days of shareholder prioritization at the cost of other important values such as **"ecological stability"** has shifted dramatically over the years. The explosion of globalisation, advanced technologies, and expansion in sociocultural, socioeconomic and geopolitical borders has found us in a place where as a greater collective we are demanding for organisations to carry deeper levels of transparency in the business activities, be more inclusive in their actions and carry a longer-term vision for their business practices.

With this shift in consciousness in mind, what can we expect from businesses now and in the future? When we ask ourselves this question, what we are really asking is: "what are our collective values? What will we tolerate as a society from global business and what level of responsibility are we all playing at"? With that in mind and heart, let's explore 2 ways that businesses can expand their impact and presence in the world in a healthy and positive way.

1.   Social Contribution

We want more. We want to know and even visibly see that our consumer dollars are contributing to worthy causes **beyond our requirement** to satisfy an immediate product purchase. Today's consumer is not only looking at the quality of the product, they are looking at the ethos and **ethics of a company**. Are they contributing and sharing their profits? Are there clear giveback mechanisms and systems in place?

Is the organisation thinking about the land and its people? Are they making an impact in the world that is positive, healthy and healing?

This level of **extended wealth creation** and equity based-thinking is creating opportunities for groups of people around the world that would once not be possible. Ethnotek is an example where they are engaging villagers around the world to create hand-crafted traditional bags and accessories that are also

sustainable in the materials used and practical.

2.   Sustainable Thinking

We extract resources to make things, so that we can purchase things, so that we can thrive, feel good about ourselves and also compete with the Jones's (that is another article). Our world and wellness are defined by GDP. A measure that effectively tells us how 'happy' we are based largely on our country's expenditure, economic activity and purchasing power. Whilst there is some validity in this, we are **evolving beyond this** – it's simply a matter of time. In the interim, consumers and businesses alike are realising that we live on a planet of finite resources and rampant consumption and **irresponsible resource / energy extraction** is not viable long-term.

As consumers we are demanding the companies we share our hard-earned dollars with are being considerate, thinking long-term (generational) and eliciting business practices of longevity in the creation and distribution. We are demanding less green-washing and more transparency. Companies alike, are realising that it is not sustainable for profit margins or steady growth that they do not **consider the environment** and master new ways of **producing goods and services** that carry sustainability in their practices.

This level of interconnectedness and closed loop thinking is more inclusive, safer to the environment as it provides the Earth and opportunity to regenerate, whilst also building deeper relationships with the consumer. Patagonia is a great example of this where they are moving away from production practices such as planned obsolescence and creating **life-long products**. Are they losing revenue? The answer is no and they are **gaining raving fans**, because people are not feeling they are numbers, or objects.

3.   Values First

When an organisation knows it values and what it stands for (it's WHY), it is able to

connect with people at a deeper and very visceral level. This level of connectedness empowers consumers to really see, know and feel the company they are either purchasing from or partnering with in some way. Ultimately a level of intimacy and closeness is developed and transparency becomes the norm.

The benefits of being transparent, open and clear with organisational values is the outside world can then observe the integrity in living them through coherent business practices.

Again, we come to a place where consumer and creator are developing a mutual respect for one another that begins to grow. It is this intimate growth that inspires organisations to simply do better and do more. To leverage efficiencies, prioritise a multitude of values and be more a company that does what it says. Wholefoods are a strong example of this and in fact combine all three of the suggestions made in this article.

"The world is changing. We are no longer a world isolated, but rather a world integrated – reliant on each other now more than ever. Our choices are to embrace the interconnected nature of our world or pretend we can continue unsustainable business practices and draw from a well that is finite."- Stefanos Sinfandos ↗

YOU LIVE EVERY SINGLE DAY AND DIE ONCE

By Katrin Israel (Estonia)

People often say you live only once, but the reality is that you <u>live every single day</u> and die only once. Everyone is given the opportunity to live for a particular period of time, and the actions you take for the particular time given to you means a lot. As a matter of fact, the **result of your actions** taken while you were alive for so many days can live for years after your demise. Interestingly, it is never too late or early to **start taking shrewd actions**, for we die only once, which the time is unknown to no man. Let your actions be the one to talk for you even after the day you pass on.

Even though many are willing to take actions, some are still yet to take actions due to fear. Many are **afraid of taking actions** and **eventually are failing**. However, we need to understand that trying and failing is not a crime and neither is it a bad thing. In fact, through **the road that leads to success**, one would most likely meet failure. Failing is a **normal process** that may be encountered after taking actions, but **the bonus** is on you to strive and persevere even after failing to achieve success. If you get the opportunity to converse with successful people and ask them about failure, they most definitely have a lot to discuss about the subject based on **personal experiences**. This proves that even highly successful people are not new to failure. A successful person is simply someone who failed but never gave up. The **difference between a successful person and a failure** is that one succumbed to trying times. This is why no one is worthy to be called a failure, except the person accepts to have failed and never intends to try again or take further actions.

It would be unreasonable to talk about success without talking about mentality. Mentality is one of the major factors that determines success, and for this reason, it is crucial for you to positively shape your mentality. Arguably, successful people and failures have different mentality. While **successful people believe that challenges are bound to arise** and be tackled, failures give up at the slightest challenge. Successful people take actions, while failures give excuses on why they have not taken actions. One remarkable trait of successful people that is worth emulating is that they do not really believe in the term "fail," so they rather interchange it with "learn." They believe that for every goal you take actions to achieve, you either win or learn. Rather than admitting that they have failed, they say they have learnt, which they have truly learnt one or two things that will be used as guideline for their further actions.

One of the best advices that exists in this world is" never be afraid." You are similar to millions of other people who are also afraid of taking actions, and the only thing that will make you a stand-out is **your ability to get rid of your fear** and take an action forthwith. There is not even a single reason why you should be afraid of failure. Take an action today that will change your life for good. You will be surprised that the action you have been reluctant to take all these while is the precise thing needed to make amazing things start happening in your life. Do not be afraid to go outside of your comfort zone when it is necessary to make you **achieve the success** you crave for.

One thing many are guilty of is cogitating too much about what the end result of our actions will be. This is exactly what brings fear the most. It is good to project for the future, but when we excessively put our focus on what the outcome of our actions will be, we are liable to lose focus of the necessary things of the present. We gradually lose focus on the things we have control over, which could even influence the outcome of our actions. If you spend more of your time being worried about the possible outcome of your actions in the next 12 months, you would most likely miss out on the actions that could be taken right now that would improve whatever you are currently working on. The past is unchangeable and **the future is undeterminable**, so it is only wise for you to pay more focus on the present that you have control over. Interestingly, when your present is accurately handled, your negative pasts becomes insignificant and you can also rest assured that your future will turn out positively.

Personally, I believe there is nothing more regrettable that living for so many days, dying just one day, and ending up not making any impact. It is quite execrable when even thought of. ✦

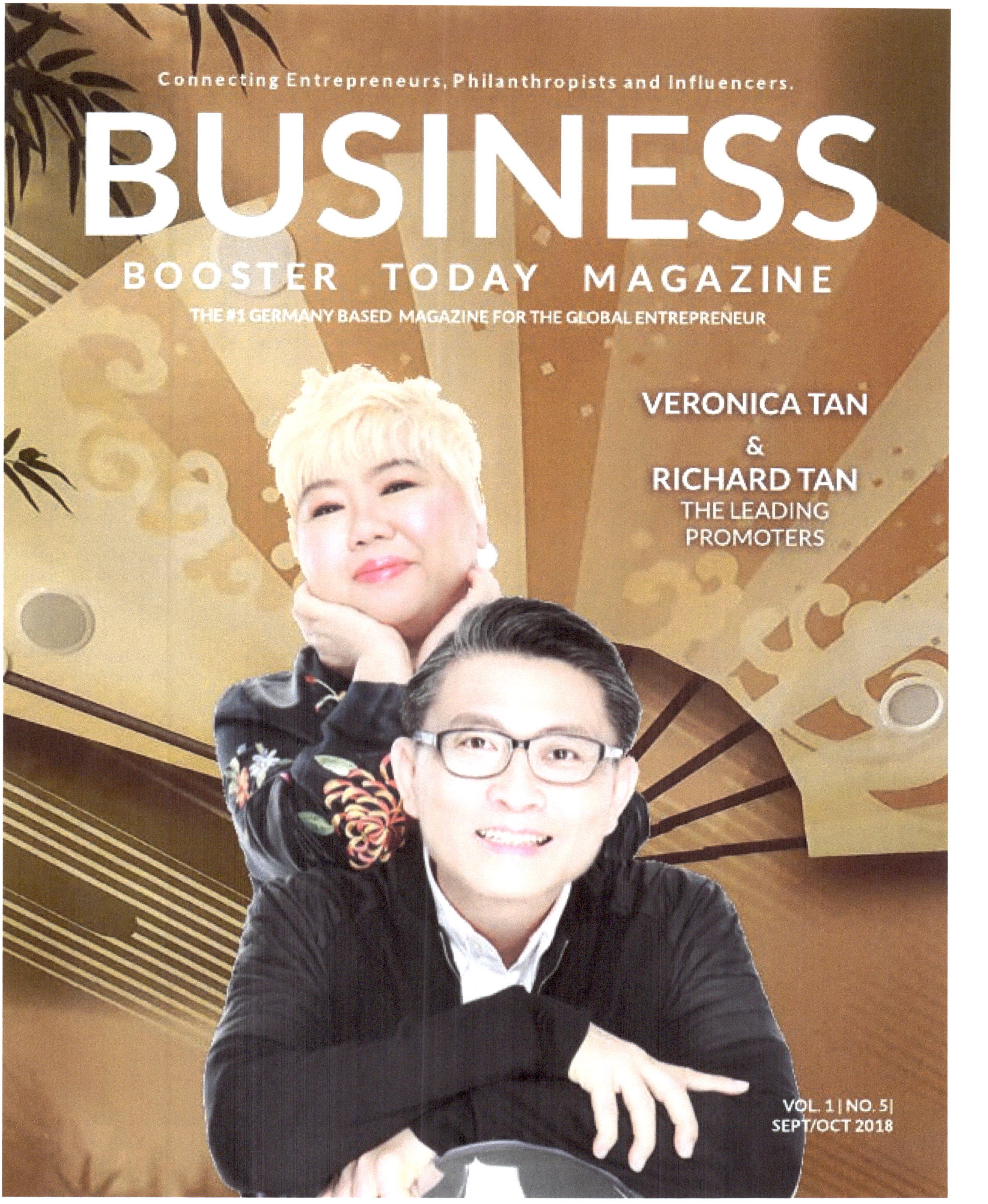

Connecting Entrepreneurs, Philanthropists and Influencers.

BUSINESS
BOOSTER TODAY MAGAZINE
THE #1 GERMANY BASED MAGAZINE FOR THE GLOBAL ENTREPRENEUR

VERONICA TAN

&

RICHARD TAN
THE LEADING
PROMOTERS

VOL. 1 | NO. 5|
SEPT/OCT 2018

THE STORY BEHIND SHREDRACK — THE MOST USEFUL INFLATABLE CAR ROOF

By Tobi Deckert (Germany)

It all started with the simple need of transporting big sport gear while traveling, especially by plane. Once arriving at your destination's airport, increasing the size of a rental car, simultaneously increases the amount of money one has to spend. For the simple reason to transport all the gear? An easier and cost-effective solution had to be found…

The **idea of ShredRack** was born, a **lightweight and modular car roof rack** which is **inflatable**!

When **Tobi came to Norway with his friends** for the first time, they had a lot of ski and snowkite gear with them. The reason for this was one of the hardest snowkite events in the world, the "RedBull Ragnarok". 300 people racing with skis dragged by their kites along a 25 km course. It is obvious that strategy and the right gear plays an important role in this game.

If you don't have a week to travel to and through Norway by car in order to reach the beautiful **National Park Haugastøl** in which the competition takes place, a plane and a rental car are the best solutions. As the van sized cars cost about 3-4 times the amount of a usual business car, the idea of ShredRack was born.

With 5 years of experience in the development of inflatable products such as event tents and kites, **Tobi used his engineering skills** to come up with the idea of building an inflatable car roof rack, which should be easy to use and fit on any car size. Back home he spends months on the sewing and welding machines to build one prototype after another. Finally, he was able to define a **special design of the ending of the air tube** in order to be able to pump the air inside within seconds — and this without an external pump. **Immediately patented**, next steps could be done…

> "During my journeys to different sports competitions all over Europe, I always had trouble to take all gear with me. A small sized roof rack quickly inflated on the rental cars roof was the necessary solution. The ShredRack was born"- **Tobi Deckert**

One year later it was done. Four people, three board bags and one car. With their mission on exploring Norway's glaciers, the four friends put all the bulky gear on the roof of their car. With specially designed straps (waterproof and anti-slip coated) they were able to put either the bags or their gear directly on the racks when hitting for their next adventure. Driving along the Lofoten through heavy rain and snow falls **with temperatures of -20°** was kind of the proof of concept of this nice little new product.

After this very successful experience the company was founded in 2017 in order to prepare final tests and materials for mass production. A lot of legal issues were discussed and also for **product compliance and liability institutions** like TÜV, the final decision was easier than expected: as the ShredRack roof rack is not connected to the car by screws, only **the driver is responsible for securing the payload**. So, it is legal to drive with an inflated car roof rack on your roof.

High quality materials play an important role when it comes to textile products that should **fulfill technical requirements**. Therefore, the most important material, the inside bladder which keeps the air is being

car. This rack is not filled with air but rather plastic bottles or towels. A similar concept effectively used.

The future of this practical oriented brand from Germany is simple: making life easier with genius, German engineered, products in the section of sports, traveling and nature. Therefore, **another brand called "tronature" www.tronature.com has been founded** to bring well thought about and similar multi-functional products into the backpacking industry as well. Our lives are becoming more and more hectic.

The **trend of exploring the world** in a simple way and even working remotely from different places is the world will become a more and more serious topic among employees. In order to fulfill this

sourced in Germany. Also, the welding process for the bladders — with specially designed tools — are made in Germany. When it comes to the final assembly the team of ShredRack decided to cooperate with "**Stiftung Liebenau**" a workspace which gives an opportunity to disabled people in order to take part in the productive economy and job life.

So far so good, the production process was on and it was time for marketing. Due to his **extreme sport lifestyle** with Skiing, kitesurfing and paragliding, Tobi started building up a team and the interest of more and more people began to arise. This was also the moment when <u>the first ShredRacks mounted with skiing, surfing and kiteboarding gear were traveling through the world</u> to make their riders happy at the most beautiful spots on this planet. Some exhibitions followed and soon their own webshop www.shredrack.com

created first sales after the official launch in summer 2018.

In the meantime, the team of ShredRack is also proud of their green product award in which they have been selected in 2018. Due to the fact that more people can go together with their gear fitting in one car instead of using two cars, it was worth spreading this concept. Also, the product range has been enlarged, that customers with big Stand up paddle boards or Kayaks are able to fit their toys on their car roof. With the ShredRack prime, **the weight of the payload can be spread more easily on the roof** and special materials allow similar lightweight. On the other hand, ShredRack mini is the solution for low budget seeking surfers who only want to fit one or two of their boards on the

wish of freedom and being able to live this adventure, the team of ShredRack is working hard on their next generation's product. Stay excited about it!

Connect with Tobi Deckert, CEO of Shred Rack GmbH at: www.tobideckert.de

Find out more about Shred Rack and their products here: www.shredrack.com

↗

EXCLUSIVE INTERVIEW WITH MICHAEL KUZILNY (AUSTRALIA)

By Sue Baumgaertner-Bartsch (Germany)

Dear Michael, you are a Multi-award-winning motivational speaker, TV presenter, legal commentator and one of the best-known criminal defence lawyers in Australia. How did you become the owner of one of Australia's most successful law firms?

I have always had a passion to help others through the tough times. Life is tough for all of us, and when you lose yourself in the service of others, without always thinking about how much money you are going to make, **life seems to flow nicely**, and success comes naturally. I am very grateful to be able to **help people get their life's back on track**, and I am grateful daily. I also believe integrity and kindness is extremely important in life and in business. If we are 100 per cent honest with all **our thoughts and actions**; the universe seems to bring great opportunities to us. Life does really have a perfect accounting system; what we put out, comes back with abundance.

Why did you get into criminal law?

There are many people in life I look up to, my father John and Vera, my mentors, and the men and woman who have dedicated themselves to the service of others; without being concerned about the opinions of others. **Nelson Mandela** has been a great inspiration in my life. He lived a **fearless and courageous life**. He was a man of integrity who fought for social justice, to make sure people and society are not overly controlled by society and governments.

A lot of governments around the world impose rules and regulations to make us dumb, sick and broke. If we all act like sheep and don't speak up when things or laws are simply wrong; then we will always be like sheep. I think it's important to not always conform to the norms of society. Society does not always get it right. I remember growing up in Hamburg, West Germany when the wall still divided the West from the East. When I was 9; my family and I were having lunch near the border, and I remember watching border guards beat, detain and arrest a family trying to flee to the west, to have a better, free life. I asked my parents why they were so brutal and nasty, to punish people for coming to the other side. They replied, "That's just the way it is." On the news over the years I saw countless people trying to live a free life, being detained or killed by these border guards who were simply told what to do by the current government. Years later the laws were changed, and these border guards were charged with manslaughter; and many went to jail. We cannot always accept what the media or our governments tell us to do, we need powerful, fearless people in the world who question rules; laws and regulations; to ensure society is protected.

The more successful you become, the more media attention you get but also the more you are prone to false allegations. We see for example, celebrities, business people and business coaches and speakers like Tony Robbins in the news of sexual allegations and other allegedly inappropriate behaviour. Claims as such can affect your family life, your business, your ability to travel and more importantly your freedom. What is your viewpoint on potentially fake claims, the media and dealing with allegations?

When you speak out, and deal with so many people over the decades, there will always be the odd person who makes a complaint or is simply unhappy with our service. I learnt over the years, that you cannot make everyone happy, and be a people pleaser. The **haters,** **the backstabbers, the complainers and the naysayers** will always be in attack mode, and often it is something wrong in their life's; and they seem to find something wrong with everyone and everything. If we know we are doing our best every day, work honestly and with full integrity, then we should have an attitude where we become independent of the good opinions of other people. When I give legal comment in the National media, whether in print or speaking about a legal topic or high-profile case on TV; I receive hundreds of emails; mostly positive, with viewers saying how they were inspired, and that they love the work I do in the community. Then there is the odd email from the jealous competitor, or the anonymous hater, who will call me all sorts of names. The more successful we become, and the more we appear in the media, the more we become a target for the haters. If we look at people like Donald Trump, we can see mental toughness. There are so many negative stories appearing in the media, and the hate pages about him. But then there are thousands of positive stories of success and achievement about him, which blow the naysayers out of the water. We need to have strong minds and ignore the people in life who want to put us down. There will always be bullies in life, whether at school, in the workplace or even amongst friends. Life is too short for useless acquaintances.

You are also an international success coach and speaker, who loves to motivate small and large companies, (FORTUNE 500) companies, to achieve increased happiness, productivity and work /life balance. Why?

I believe Western society is becoming increasingly unstable and unhappy. Depression rates, and suicide rates around the world are substantially increasing. Millions of people around the world are resorting to anti-depressants to cover up their inner problems. **My passion to become a global high performance / motivational speaker**, was to inspire companies, team leaders, and their employees to realize the impermanence of life. We are all going to die. Life is short, and life is here to be enjoyed, to be happy, and not to just chase materialism. So many people are chasing all the toys of life, are trying to impress others with their beautiful cars and homes. These things are certainly important, and are a sign of a successful life, but we should also have spiritual life. I talk a lot about meditation in my talks, it's one of the most important things we can do daily, and we will see success come naturally. A calm mind brings a happy life. If our minds are turbulent; no matter how much money, we have in the bank; our life's will be mostly unhappy. I teach people in a very simple way how to mediate and how it will change their life's. I also believe life is 10 per cent what happens, and 90 per cent how we react to it. In my talks around the globe, I remind people that we are all suffering in one way or another. There is always something going on in our life's we are not happy with. From my many years being on the front line of law enforcement, I speak about the importance of learning to deal with crises.

FAKE SECURITY GUARD
HE ILLEGALLY CARRIED A HANDGUN AT MALL MEMORIAL

must do whatever it takes to bring our dreams and goals to life. We have to be fearless, and unstoppable. Not just sometimes, but we have to be committed and determined to take massive action every day. You have to be prepared to do whatever it takes; and not be concerned what "the others" may think. Consistency is important. WE have to have the heart of a lion, not a sheep. There are far too many sheep in the world today.

How do you stay motivated and what keeps you going?

Every day I wake up I am grateful with all the areas of my life. The way I start my mornings are very important. It sets the tone of the day to come. I wake up at 5am every morning and commence my "hour of power". 20 minutes of mediation followed by 40 minutes of exercise and going over my goals for the day. I tend to live in day tight compartments, and every day for me is a fresh start, with new exiting opportunities. The past is the past, and the future is a mystery we don't need to be concerned about today. Today is a super fantastic day with lots of wonderful things that will happen to you! We also have to realize that life doesn't give you want, life gives you what you deserve. Sometimes we just have to give up control and go with the flow of life.

Michael, throughout your legal and media career, you have met people at a point where the impacts of a split-second decision can result in either victory or vulnerability. Tell us about your new book "Split second".

SPLIT SECOND is an authentic journey about my 30-year career in the criminal justice system. The book is all about my life journey, the corruption I faced as a law enforcer, the good, the bad, and the ugly. In SPLIT SECOND I share my own insecurities and fears as a young cop. I speak about Australia's worst massacre that I attended, how I came face to face with a serial killer, and how I saw some police officers take the wrong path and end up behind bars. The

book shares my journey how I had to develop a strong mind, and the importance of courage. The book is all about life and the choices we make. There are no free lunches in life. If we give love, love comes back. If we are kind to others, others will be kind to us. If we speak about others behind their back, criticise and always find fault with others, that's what will come back in abundance. I really believe that life is a game of boomerangs; what we give out, always comes back.

What is one of your the scariest "split second" business decisions you have ever faced?

When I started meditation 20 years ago, the fear, the worry, the so-called scary stuff all faded away. I don't do negative, and I have become fearless and independent towards the opinions of others. I remind myself daily, that in 240 months we will be 20 years older. Life is simple, and there is no such thing as stress; only people having stressful thoughts.

What is the next "big thing" that you are working on (in your business)?

I love to inspire people around the world through the law, through my speaking engagements, and through the media. For many years I enjoyed hosting a national show called "Tough times never Last". I interviewed thousands of authentic and beautiful people who fearlessly shared their life journey, and the tough times they faced. This in turn inspired viewers how to face their tough times. I am presently working Television project of a similar nature, that will inspire viewers globally. There are 7 billion of us. We all face tough times. The more people I can influence and inspire around the globe to live happier and more successful life's, the happier I will be. Life is beautiful full of beautiful people! ✐

MICHAEL KUZILNY
Legal Affairs Editor
CAN 17° LONDON: HEIGHTENED SECURITY AT MARATHON   8:11   live

TOUGH TIMES NEVER LAST
with Michael Kuzilny

What does success mean to you and what do you need to succeed in business?

Success for me is everything I do and say. Success for me is integrity and having a strong mind and a strong life. Success for me is taking winning actions daily and saying no to the things that take me away from my journey. Success is also realizing that life is a test, and that we are all perfectly imperfect. As long as we learn from those mistakes and move on with life; you will achieve an incredible life. To succeed in business, we

HOW SALES FUNNELS DRIVE LEADS INTO YOUR BUSINESS

By Christian Bartsch (Germany)

When it comes to generating revenue companies have to **first attract leads** towards their offers. This applies for online companies and local businesses, too. If you can not get people into your premises (online or physical), you can not **close deals** with these buyers.

This is where marketing and sales go hand in hand by applying the **sales funnel strategy**. this is what we do to generate leads for our different areas of business. Sales funnels can be via **online and offline funnel pathways**.

Depending on your target audience you might have to go old school in order to get your leads into your online world. We use **our own lead research tool** that is able to **generate target lists** so that we can use this for online advertising, cold calling and offline advertising.

People often mistake a *distribution of printed leaflets via letter boxes* as the ultimate tactic to generate leads. Unfortunately, the reality is that these kind of **outdated marketing tools** are highly disengaged from the target audience. The closer your target audience gets to the **millennial demographic section** the worse an outdated marketing tactic will fail.

Even online sales funnels need to be more than static picture advertising. I have been advertising my business services and products via google ads and Facebook ads. When you **hire advertising agencies** you would expect great results, but reality is that this will not always drive your invested cash back into your account. I have tested agencies that claim to have fantastic **artificial intelligence** system that tweek your ads so that they are super powerful and dirt cheap. Well, they failed to

generate any leads and the costs were crazy high. Eventually my ads performed better during the same test period and generated sales at a far lower cost that the non-lead generating ads could achieve.

> *"We need to be aware of the fact that a sales funnel strategy does not just consist of an advertising image and a landing page. It is a combination of a sales processes, **social awareness**, marketing, **psychology**, copy writing, **tactical design**, email marketing, **customer lifecycle concepts** and more",* Christian Bartsch.

Modern sales funnels consist of images that are focused on the **core behavioral characteristics of audiences** - whether they are male or female - and even age can be a critical element that you need to address when trying to get people to engage with your advertising. This can even be extended to the use of videos that have special scripts for collecting audience samples.

Once you have gained leads that are interested in your lead magnet offer or events then, you need to keep them entertained. Yes, you have to **ensure they do not forget that you exist**. At the same time you need to be unreasonable with the quantity of engagement and the way you attempt to connect with your target audience. Do it the wrong way and you will fail.

Having branding in place can help boost the credibility of your offers. Unfortunately some entrepreneurs and companies believe they

have got a good branding. The fact that they do **not know how to apply the branding** in their *marketing, sales and recruitment process* is just one of their key issues that leads to failure.

Our in-house consultants and experts have been trained and certified for a multitude of platforms. This is absolutely necessary, as with today's diversity of systems needed for a **sales funnel life cycle** you need more than just a lead page and an email application.

Customers who engage with our magazine customer service will see that we have special dedicated mail servers, a CRM system with email automation, a variety of landing page platforms and membership management systems. We even use a tool that can automatically send out SMS text messages world wide to our selected clients. Want an extra topping? Yep, you can even use chat bots to **increase the engagement** and **boost your conversion rates**.

Unfortunately, many entrepreneurs try a platform, and advertising system or other tools believing it will solve their problems. They eventually burn cash and do a miserable attempt at using the opportunities. That is when they claim advertising does not work or it is a scam by big corporations. That is all humbug due to ignorance and unwillingness to do what is necessary so that a marketing campaign can be successful.

Those who use our **3 step system** have a shortcut to success. This is not for everyone. ✐

You can reach the author at chris@thesuccesscreators.com

Connecting Entrepreneurs, Philanthropists and Influencers.

BUSINESS

BOOSTER TODAY MAGAZINE

THE #1 GERMANY BASED MAGAZINE FOR THE GLOBAL ENTREPRENEUR

STEVE MARABOLI
THE MOST QUOTED
MAN ALIVE

ANIMATION
NOW AND THEN

SALES
STRATEGIES

VOL. 2 | NO. 5|
MAY/JUNE 2019

"INNOVATION WILL ALWAYS WIN"

STEVE JOBS

By Yelena Ganshof (Switzerland)

Across all the media we constantly hear about blockchain, artificial intelligence, cryptocurrencies, augmented reality, and we wonder what it is all about. For those working in technology, all these terms are very familiar now, while for others – particularly industrialists – it is a Wonderland. The only thing we know is that we are on the edge of a big technological revolution. And the main question for all the professionals and business owners is where we are going, what to expect and how to adjust our businesses to all these technological changes.

As a producer and host of **INSIDE TOMORROW TV** talk show, I have guests speaking on their fascinating projects based at innovation hub in Switzerland and abroad. So, let me open a curtain of Inside Tomorrow for you and be your Alice in this Wonderland.

A few core technologies developing today are:

ARTIFICIAL INTELLIGENCE and machine learning become an integral part of our lives. AI applications now are not only recognizing data, languages, voice and images, they help us analyze all these documents and collect into reports. Face Recognition is a great application example used in security and criminology. AI also help write articles in multiple languages and be our personal assistant and editor. The goal here is to let AI do the routine part (faster and more efficient) leaving creative and controlling part for human beings.

BLOCKCHAIN was initially created to serve a public transaction ledger of cryptocurrency Bitcoin. Basically, the invention of the first cryptocurrency was to solve the double -spending problem, reduce costs and increase efficiency between the accounting parties. Started with cryptocurrencies, the technology initially found its application in Banking and Fintech to speed up back office settlements for asset management, insurance claims processing, cross-border payments. Now

YELENA GANSHOF
PRODUCER AND HOST
INSIDE TOMORROW

blockchain is spreading into all kinds of business applications which needs control of transactions such logistics, tangible and intangible property, healthcare (personal health records with confidentiality access), music (ownership rights, royalty distribution) and government (elections and personal identity). Reveling personal data is a very sensitive issue today based on what happened at Facebook, and this is where blockchain technology can come very handy to make our data protected and encrypted, sharing this information only with relevant people we choose at certain times.

AUGMENTED REALITY is an interactive experience of a real-world environment where the objects residing in the real-world are augmented or enhanced by computer-generated images and information. Google Maps AR has been first demonstrated in 2018 and teased the world in early 2019. This application allows us to help navigate when walking. It points us in the right direction and gives information about the buildings and shops around. The first commercial introduction of AR happened in gaming and entertainment. Remember the SnapChat? Microsoft and Magic Leap have used the technology to move from gaming to industry with their Mixed Reality headsets.

Early 2019 in Switzerland, BOBST launched the first ever remote assistance service in the packaging industry to incorporate a smart headset with AR glasses. Customers asking technical assistance can wear the smart headset and connect with experts who can simultaneously see what the user sees and advice in real time. Vifor Pharma implemented AR system in its manufacturing systems and packaging. Wearing a headset, floor operators adapt printed manuals into continuous real-life checklist they see in their glasses. According to the recent research, 100 million people will shop with AR by 2020.

5G: Government, companies and consumers are all in between preparing to trade out 4G wireless infrastructure for 5G. This will allow users enhance download speeds by 15 times faster than the global average now. It would also allow autonomous cars to "speak" between each other and boost the market development. 5G is a network of networks or a system of systems, and the satellites will become an integral part in this equation. Amazon has now entered this area with plans to launch more than 3,000 satellites with a vision to provide low-latency, high-speed broadband connectivity to many communities around the globe. Basically, the space is on the turning point from the stage of research

and discovery into the stage of commercialization.

Whether you work in medicine or arts, real estate or finance, you always need to come up with new ideas and new applications to keep your business viable and agile to new technologies. Medicine is already going through drastic changes applying robotics in surgery, AI in diagnostics, AR in pharmaceuticals, 3D printing in individual dosage of pills. We as humans all want to be healthier, look younger and stay longer in shape. Technology is now giving us this opportunity of shifting us from Humans to Augmented Humans. So, what's next?

Join us at INSIDE TOMORROW to see what the future will be made of.

Producer and Host: INSIDE TOMORROW
Innovation & Technology
(Dukascopy TV, Geneva Switzerland)
Founder of VAIVA.ch and
BrandBoosting.com ✐

SELLING DEALS TO INVESTORS

By John Stokoe (United Kingdom)

STEP FIVE - SOURCING THE DEAL

How do I find investors?

So now you've got your investment area, you've found a cracker of a deal and it's all priced and packaged up ready to go. Now you need someone to sell it to. Just as any business, the key to a successful, ongoing business is finding quality individuals and investors to source to. You want to build up a database of quality investors that you can source deals to quickly and efficiently.

There are plenty of 'armchair investors' out there; people who prefer a hands-off approach to investing. The trick here is finding them, building credibility and spending the time to build genuine rapport.

You will also need to do a little of your own due diligence on them; as much as they are trying to get to know you, this is also your opportunity to get a feel for them. You want to know that you can work together and that they will hold up their end of the deal. You'll have to ensure they have the funding they say they do, and are ready to go when the deal can proceed.

Current Network

First of all, tap into your current resources. If you already invest in property yourself, it's like you have a network of people around you. Keep a source pack of a current or previous deal to hand at all times, and you'd be surprised by how many people request to see it once you start talking. Most people are fed up with the 0.5% - 1% they can earn in the bank and would love to have an income-generating property. They just may not have the inclination, time or knowledge to do so – you do.

Friends and Family

The same goes again for your friends and family. You make people money; be proud of

that. Share your journey with the people around you, help them understand how your business works and the returns people are seeing, and they too will want to invest themselves.

Networking Events

Local business and property networking events are a great place to meet new investors; particularly those who may be cash rich, but time poor. A lot of individuals who would like to get into property attend these meetings, and again may not have the time or experience that you do. This is exactly when you can offer value. If you have great deals to offer, there will be someone at these networking events who wants to buy them. Websites such as Eventbrite and Meetup are a great place to find upcoming meetings.

Online

For finding quality investors, online platforms including your website and social media such as Facebook and LinkedIn prove to be incredibly useful tools. It is crucial that you and your business has an online presence; in the modern digital era looking a company up online is often how we ascertain its credibility. Use Facebook and other digital platforms to showcase you, your brand and what you offer. Post before and after pictures of the deals you have worked on, ask current clients to provide you a testimonial and engage with the people who follow you. When you then post a great deal, you'll have the investors coming to you.

Source My Property Investor Database

The importance of a quality investor database cannot be stressed enough. This is your income source; these are your clients. Over the years, working alongside some other quality sourcing agents, we've experienced how difficult this step can be. We recognised that for us all to be successful we needed to pull our resources. And that's exactly what we

did.

Source My Property is now a well-recognised brand and sourcing agents who we work with closely can become an accredited SMP sourcing partner. This gives them access to our nationwide SMP investor database. SMP work together as a team to answer any questions to ensure more deals are sold. We also share our deals amongst us so we can select the very best that are available.

At Source My Property Academy, we offer comprehensive training in how to get your sourcing business up and running. We've pulled together all of our experience, drawing on fantastic opportunities – and biggest mistakes – to help others who want to become sourcing agents learn how to do this the right way, from the very beginning. We emphasise the need for professionalism and integrity, but we also show our partners how they can make some serious money in this business, and enjoy every second of building it.

For more details on this process we run a Sourcing academy :
https://www.sourcemyproperty.com/academy/

MY FEAR OF FAILURE STARTED WITH A HAMBURGER COMMERCIAL

By Jim Paar (USA)

Hi, my name is Jim Paar, founder of Paar Media Group and Up2Paar. From being a child actor in Hollywood to Restaurant Owner of 3 restaurants and many other ventures, I now own a very successful international marketing agency and helped brand some of the most successful businesses in the world. I have worked with many leading brands such as Michelin, Bosch, Kimberly Clark, Paramount Pictures, Indy Racing Series, and many more.

Early Beginnings

Like many successful entrepreneurs. My life has been layered with many failures. My entrepreneurship began when I was six months old. My parents entered my twin brother and me into our first baby food commercial. This was the start of our acting career.

By the time I was seven years old, I landed an audition for a hamburger commercial. It was a very simple task to take a bite of a hamburger and we would have closed the deal. I didn't want to eat the hamburger and refused to eat the hamburger much to the anger and disappointment of the four adults in that audition room. In short, we didn't land the commercial.

Looking back that decision negatively impacted me for years, I felt that I let my family down and that somehow, I had to repay them for that "mistake". It would have been easier to say "yes", that could have launched our career in the acting business and became successful. Maybe saying no actually paved our way for other successes.

By the time I was 18 I left my home in Minnesota on an adventure of different opportunities. I became the jack of all trades and yet tried to master them all with no consistency. I was a Paramedic, Life Flight Medic, SWAT team member, General Contractor, International importer, and many other businesses which led to three restaurants. The irony of all this is that I was into everything that brought me into many moments of nothingness. "That failure turned out to be the gifts I needed".

My First Big Failure as an Adult

In 2005 the National Hockey League went on strike that lasted over 10 months, this led to me suffering financial losses due to the proximity of my one restaurant close to the hockey arena. Despite what was evident, my ego proved that I could overcome. This led to me selling all my restaurants.

You see, the fear of failure and embarrassment kept me imprisoned from making the right business decisions when the strong evidence already presented when the strike started happening. I walked away feeling like I completely failed but somehow did my best moving forward.

The Next Big Failure

Only two weeks after the restaurant closures, I started a new business, Portable Media. I got the attention of the PGA (Professional Golf Association) and eventually started selling advertisement for these media placements. During this time just as I was on the road to success another huge setback happened, this time to a costly tune of almost $250,000 in litigation fees. Emotionally exhausted, mentally drained, and almost physically caved in from the court trial battling to protect my patents. The end was a settlement, that's right, I settled instead of taking this to the finish line. Personally, I felt like a failure because I felt like I gave up on my own dreams.

Lesson #1 - Lessons from These Failures

Would I said "Yes" to the hamburger there would have been a great possibility of having our successful commercial.

Just like many struggling artists, they never get to hear from Hollywood again. My brother and I could have been a statistic. This is what happened to River Phoenix with the mental breakdowns, a lot of young Hollywood celebrities go through and the one hit wonders. I am glad I said "no" to the hamburger.

Lesson #2 – If You Fail To Plan, Plan To Fail." – Ben Franklin

When I was young, I went from creating one business to another to another without a clear direct plan with a lot of ego. Needless to say, it was also followed by one failure after another. Whether you're in entrepreneurship or corporate it is critical to have clear strategies, mentors, coaches, and ongoing personal development with a clear structure. Trust me, you'd save yourself years of defeat. "A pilot never takes flight without a flight plan, and neither should you".

Lesson #3 – Have a Clear Structure to Your Day

My day starts at 4:30 am every day on the dot. I start with prayer and devotions, then off to the gym, and then my MIT's (Most Important Task). It helps keep me stay focused when distractions present themselves. Have a clear and results-oriented game plan.

Final Lesson

In my life, there is a God. When I was backed through all these "failures" and the many times I questioned if God really existed during those times, the answer is "yes". Because those failures were the foundation I needed, to have achieved what I have today.

It would be egotistical of me to think I did this on my own. Of course, I have to take massive action but there were also a lot of prayers that had been said, especially at times the challenges were strongly present and he had never failed me yet.

I wish you success in your life. Remember failures are not setbacks, they are a setup for something greater. ✒

CRITICISM AND TOXIC PEOPLE

By Douglas Vermeeren (Canada)

All of us have experienced people that have been less than enthusiastic and support about what we are doing and who we trying to be. You've probably heard these people referred to as toxic or critics. No one likes negative people in our lives. Many of the the gurus suggest that you need to eliminate as many toxic people from your life as you can and focus only on positive people.

Often one of the questions I get from those I teach is: what did you observe with the world's top achievers? How did they eliminate toxic people from their lives?

The answer: They didn't. In fact, all top achievers have negative people and influences in their lives, but the reason why they are successful isn't because they run from these people or shun them. They actually learn how to manage them better.

In fact, you cant run from problems, challenges or negativity if you expect to create success.

Instead you need to learn how to rise above it or in the case of people in some circumstances you need to have your vision so powerful that they are inspired to get with the program and become supportive.

A quote I shared on social media not too long ago applies here. Give your haters so much value that they change their mind.

Now there definitely are some toxic people I am going to recommend you spend less time with them and you certainly don't let their thinking influence you. But I am not going to go to the unsafe or unproductive extreme where some gurus are recommending severing ties with family members or getting a divorce. While its true that sometimes divorce is the answer you might want to be careful about rushing into something like that. Just because a person is asking you to be realistic or pointing or some things that you could improve doesn't mean you shouldn't listen.

So lets talk a little bit about a few different kinds of people that are often thought of as negative or critical so you can recognize the useful ones.

Let's divide them into two categories for our discussion today. Complainers and critics. I believe there are often categories too <u>where people are just downright mean and cruel</u>. But I want to focus on the ones you may be tempted to listen to.

First it is important to point out the goal of complainers and critics. This will be helpful for you to understand. When you know their goal then you can **recognize your position** and what you need to do to protect it or level yourself up as you'll see in a minute.

The goal of a complainer or critic is simply to persuade you to their point of view. In the case of the complainer you've heard the saying that says misery loves company. In the case of the critic they are trying to get you to see something that they think would improve you.

So the first line of defence is to remember that if you really are committed to your mission you must decide that you won't be swayed by the complainers and if the critic has some value you've got to be willing to receive feedback.

It reminds me a few years ago I was asked when someone has a goal what is the difference between tenacity and stupidity? Imagine someone in a room trying to get into the room next door. The stupid person bangs his head on the wall and when that doesn't works he continues banging his head again and again in exactly the same place hoping to get to the next room.

The tenacious person will also start by banging his head on the wall but when that doesn't work he tries a new spot again and again until he finds a window or a door or someone points it out to him.

In other words the big difference between a stupid persona and a tenacious person isn't the size of their goal. Its how teachable they are in getting to that goal.

So when a critic comes along we might find value and **stay teachable** before immediately shutting that person off.

I believe that both critics and complainers are sent to test us what kind of person we are and to see how committed we are to our goals. Do you really want it? Do you really believe it? Are you willing to learn? Or are you going to **stay stuck** banging your head against a wall?

So lets talk about complainers for a minute. Complainers are different than critics. Complainers often have very little to offer in terms of improvement. They often come from a place of frustration, jealousy, comparisons and ego.

I'll say that again **frustration, jealousy, compares or ego**. They are quick to point out faults but have no solutions that would make something better. I once encountered a complainer who thought he was a critic. He could quickly point out the mistakes and shortcomings of others but when I asked him if he had any solutions or something better to offer he had nothing left to say.

A critic on the other hand is generally someone who has good advice. But what makes them a critic is that they don't know how to **express the suggestion in a tactful or sensitive way**. In other words a critic is generally poorly expressed support or facts.

So here's a warning about critics. Don't be too easily offended or quick to dismiss them just because they can't express or sometimes wont take the time to express their insights in a sugar coated way. And that's a blessing to you any ways.

In my life I have had people who expressed an idea in a flowery way and I smiled and dismissed it. I have also had other be very Bold with me and it hurt - but I did something about it. Both have their place and blessing.

Often your response to a critic is more of a

reflection of you rather than a reveal of the motives of the critic. Again don't be too hasty to shut them off.

Now we've talked about other criticizing us. I want to take a minute and point the finger back at us. We all like to give advice and we like to share our thoughts and opinions.

First of all which are you mostly a complainer or a critic? Do we share things because we are

frustrated? jealous? Comparing ourselves or our situation to others? And do we speak from a place of ego because we believe we are either better or lesser than someone else? Perhaps

the idea that like attracts like is happening here and you are **bringing complainers and toxic people into your life** because that is a reflection of what you are. If that is the case you can change. Awareness is the first step to change. If you notice you are a complainer stop it.

It doesn't help anyone and it doesn't build anything. Complaining without solutions never adds value or changes anything. It just creates contention, tension and friction. As I **studied the top achievers** saw many of them in situations where they faced a complainer. They did not participate. However I have seen many struggling people jump right in when their friends start to cry about the weather (which they cannot change) The behaviour of others (WHich they cannot change) The economy (which they cannot change) The actions of the government (which they cannot change) and so forth.

Focus on what you can do about something rather than what you can say about something.

And as for being a critic I know that there are times when you genuinely have something to say that could help people. Sometimes perhaps *you are not as good* as **expressing the support or suggestions** as you would like. Sometimes perhaps we even say too much or express suggestions when its not really our place to do so.

May I suggest a few questions we could ask ourselves before treading into this deep water of correction?

Ask is what I am about to say necessary?

Ask is it my place to give this correction or is there someone more appropriate Than me to share this correction?

Is this advice really that valuable?

Is it better for them to learn it on their own?

Is it hurtful for me to say it?

You'll notice that each of these questions is designed to have us **say less and correct less** often that saying more and correcting more often.

In my experience most people know when they are doing something wrong, or need to make a correction, Most people know when something isn't working. And **the universe has a special way of helping people** make these realizations on their own in a way that they aren't offended.

Try to say less, correct less and control less. These are all signs of a mature mind and leader.

Now what about those times when you absolutely have to say something.

May I make a suggestion of something that

has worked well in our family, in my business and personally for me.

Here's the formula. Before you correct seek to validate the other person and recognize what style are doing well. Surely you can find something. This allows the person to begin by being open. They know that I have **noticed good in them** and they are now more open to receive.

Then share the suggestion in a supportive way. Briefly and not as a lecture. Try and make it clear and distinct with a clear example. Perhaps you will share why it needs to be corrected and what would give a better result. (By the way if you don;'t have a suggestion on how to fix it there's really no point mentioning it any ways.)

And once you have finished conclude with support again so that you can ensure the relationship is still intact and solid.

The pattern looks like this Love - support - love.

I also feel its useful to begin the support part by using a non-confrontation phrase like, "May I make a suggestion," or "Are you open to a few ideas."

Proverbs says a soft answer turner away wrath.

When we approach people with more kindness we get cooperation. I challenge you to look at your life and identify areas when you could be less of a complainer and a critical critic. Be supportive. When people feel you are caring and kind they have more respect and consider you more valuable. ✒

A DAY WITH A BILLIONAIRE

From being a highly successful entrepreneur and investor to spending a day with Marc Lasry, American billionaire and co-owner of the NBA's Milwaukee Bucks into the billionaire mindset

Sue Baumgaertner-Bartsch (Germany) interviews Pietro Savvides (Canada)

From being a highly successful entrepreneur and investor to spending a day with Marc Lasry, American billionaire and co-owner of the NBA's Milwaukee Bucks into the billionaire mindset

Sue Baumgaertner- Bartsch, Business Booster Today VP & Lead Editor interviews Pietro Savvides.

SBB: Pietro, you are a highly successful entrepreneur and investor. You have a **background in construction**, you know how-to put-up buildings and bring them down; you look at them and assess them, either keep them, sell them or flip them, and most importantly, **you create value**.

What are some of **the key factors to look out for** when assessing real estate nowadays and how has that changed over the past 10 years?

Pietro: The key factors to look out for when assessing real estate have not changed that much, although there are several things to watch out for when investing. When looking into investing in a property, most people look at things like **revenue and expenses, location, maintenance and carrying costs, and ROI** (return on investment).

There's nothing wrong with this, I do it all the time when I have many deals to sort through. I never limit myself to one type of property like a single-family house, or a strip mall, I keep my net wide and sift and sort through deals. Great deals don't come often although you want to increase your chances by receiving many and choosing the best one that need more careful analyzing. I don't waste much time with this process, since I have several **quick elimination tricks** that I

use. For example, the first step is to evaluate the square footage of the land versus asking price. You need to have an idea of the going price for the serviced land in the area. You also need to divide the asking price by the number of doors or addresses (rentable space). The rental market price versus asking price strategy also goes for rental property.

What the tenant is actually paying versus what the market in that area is dictating. This is a great way to see if the property has potential repositioning growth. The second step is to ask yourself if the property is financeable. If it's not, I evaluate what it would cost to make it financeable and decide whether it's worth it or not. I don't buy if the property is not financeable by a conventional mortgage. I also estimate how long it would take for the property to either be flipped or financed. Lastly, I question myself on whether there is enough profit to make it worthwhile or if it will occupy to much of my time.

What has changes in past decade is that interest rates are at an all-time low. This is where people get into financial trouble. It could be a good thing for an experienced investor, yet it can be a risk for new investors and many millennials investing in real estate. Forgetting to factor in the **potential increase in interest rates can be risky**. I always keep my eye on this, when I decided to keep a property for a longer term and **remortgage**, I need to make sure the revenues will cover the expenses. Low interest rates have caused many speculators and amateur investors to saturate the real estate markets, driving prices up and reducing the amount of inventory. This has created an increase in new construction.

It can be cheaper to build a new property rather than buying an existent one and investing more money in renovating it.

Real estate is a great vehicle for wealth building, although it can take a great deal of time, in fact even decades. There are times real estate is better short term and other times it is more profitable to buy and hold long term. I look for areas that have great potential growth in the near future, such as a new public rail system that the city or gov't is planning to build, a new bridge connecting new areas, a new highway, or even a developer that wants to **develop a deteriorated section of the city**. I will leave you with one more, government spending is at an all-time high, city's always run out of money and are always looking for new ways to increase taxes. One way they are doing this is by keeping more people in the city. They already started changing zoning in certain areas around towns. For Example, areas that have single family houses are rezoned to multi family. Land is always worth more when you can build higher. All these are some examples that can drive real estate prices through the roof. You need to be on the lookout and react sooner than later. The important factor here is to buy low and sell high. I don't purchase property hoping it appreciates 2 to 3 percent annually or buy real estate simply because I want to own real estate.

When is it a good time to sell? That's the **billion-dollar question** many ask. It's not like it used to be. Nowadays, the whole world is connected and the economy, good or bad, seems to affect everyone simultaneously. I believe a big driver of the economy is consumer spending: the more people spend the better the economy. Interest rates play a big factor in real estate as well. The higher the interest rate, the cheaper the real estate becomes. On the other hand, with lower interest rate, you can borrow more money against your property, and this causes more people to compete in the market for real estate, driving prices higher.

SBB: Pietro, people call you the "deal maker". Why do you think so many people want to work with you?

Pietro: I'm always approached by many people who want to work with me, although only a handful qualify. I've made many mistakes and gained a lot of experience that have grounded me and made me humble. I believe in **integrity, loyalty and ethical values**. In business I'm in it to win, and I try to have fun. There are many people with deals out there, all types of deals, some better than others, and some simply not worth talking about.

I believe people want to do business with me because I do what I say and say what I do.

Others simply want to work with me because they need the money to fund their project, It's definitely not my good looks. It comes down to money, the bloodline to any deal. Without capital, it's hard to get anything done.

I'm a practical guy and when I decide to work with someone on a deal, it's because I like the person, there is synergy between us and a sense of trust. I wouldn't recommend partnering with someone they don't trust, even if the deal is too good to pass.

SBB: Being a business person means meeting many different kinds of people from all walks of life. I know you have recently met **Marc Lasry**, American billionaire hedge fund manager, CEO of Avenue Capital Group and co-owner of the NBA's Milwaukee Bucks. What differentiates a millionaire's mindset from a billionaire's mindset?

Pietro: I didn't only meet him, I spent the day with him, flew with him in his private jet to Milwaukee, watched an NBA game from courtside, hung out with him in the owner's lounge, and when the game was finished, we flew back.

I'm so grateful for this experience. Marc is a true gentleman, one of a kind, friendly and a down to earth individual. Speaking to him was like speaking to my banker, I felt comfortable with him.

During the game, I had asked Marc where I could purchase shirts to bring back home with me and he quickly replied "**follow me**" and we left the court while the game was on and he brought me through a maze of corridors

and restaurants and as we went by he greeted and hugged several staff members and a few of his New York clients. He brought me up to the entrance of the Milwaukee bucks store and left me with instructions on how to get back to the game. What a class act!

Today there are a lot of millionaires, some simply became millionaires because their houses appreciated in value and surpassed the value of a million dollars, without any planning whatsoever. Most of these owners think they are the geniuses behind that. It takes more than that to be a true multi-millionaire, although I believe that one way to achieve the billionaire status is by having a great product or service that will serve many people and to do that you need to have employees that you leverage their time.

The way I plan to achieve the billionaire status is by **leveraging my investment capital** on someone else's idea and efforts. Marc told me he made it by evaluating undervalued good businesses and leveraged them for high returns, many people are doing this, although they don't all become billionaires. Mindset plays a big role.

I believe the difference between a millionaire achieving billionaire status is precise laser focus, determination and discipline. ✎

THE VIRGINIA ROBINSON GARDENS: BREATHTAKING ESTATE IN BEVERLY HILLS

By Sue Baumgaertner-Bartsch (Germany)

The Virginia Robinson Gardens is a unique historic estate set on six acres of nothing but beauty that transports the visitor back to the **birthplace of Beverly Hills**. Built in 1911, it was once the residence of retail giants Virginia and Harry Robinson and now occupies an illustrious place in history as the **first luxury estate built in Beverly Hills**.

The main house was designed in 1911 by architect Nathaniel Dryden, who was Virginia's father, in a Beaux Arts style. The residence is furnished with antiques and artifacts collected from around the world.

The twelve-room house is only one story tall – a decision that permitted most rooms to look out or open directly onto the grounds or the handsome terraces. The front door leads into a central hallway that ends at the rear of the house and the entrance to the Great Lawn. Off the central hallway – a living room, dining room, library, morning room, bedroom suite for the Robinsons, a small guest house for Virginia's mother, and a large kitchen and staff area. With their enthusiasm, the Robinsons started their **lifelong transformation** of the barren hillside into a garden paradise.

The **Renaissance Revival Pool Pavilion** was built in 1924 by architect Sumner Hunt and is modeled after the **Villa Pisani in the Tuscan region** of Italy. Decorative panels of **Sgraffito** ornamentation adorn the Roman arches at the entry to the pavilion's Solarium. The Pavilion overlooks a long pool.

The Virginia Robinson Gardens range in style and plant type from Italian Renaissance Mediterranean to Tropical. The estate has five distinctive Gardens:

- The Italian Renaissance Terrace Garden, with views of mature specimen trees and Citrus Terraces.
- The Formal Mall Garden, with perennial flower borders.
- The Rose Garden, with heirloom Roses.
- The Kitchen Garden with vegetables
- and an Herb Garden.

The Tropical Palm Garden, including a grove of Australian King Palms reportedly the largest outside Australia.

For the past thirty years, the "Friends of Robinson Gardens" have organized the annual Benefit Garden Tour to raise funds for the Virginia Robinson Gardens historical estate. Known as Beverly Hills' garden party of the year, this event is truly a **one-of-a-kind garden tour experience** as ticket holders get the opportunity to visit selected private home gardens rarely seen by the public. The affair peaks mid-day with a catered luncheon at the Virginia Robinson Gardens. Throughout the estate, ticket holders can view the mansion's historical rooms uniquely embellished by premier interior designers and florists. The luncheon program includes a fashion show of the latest looks by a top fashion brand. Guests also have the opportunity to enjoy and shop the beautiful boutique located at the covered tennis court.

The Robinson Gardens are open to the public for docent tours by advanced reservation only. This home and the gardens are simply breathtaking and are a must see.

For more information, have a look at the website:

https://www.robinsongardens.org/ ✎

BUSINESS

BOOSTER TODAY MAGAZINE

THE #1 GERMAN MAGAZINE FOR THE GLOBAL ENTREPRENEUR

INTERNATIONAL EDITION

VOL. 2 | NO. 2 | FEBRUARY 2019